Usborne Workbooks
Adding

This book belongs to

There are answers on page 27, and notes
for grown-ups at the back of the book.

Here are some of the woodland animals
you'll meet in this book. Trace over the
numbers on their leaves.

Stripe the badger

1
one
•

Olly the owl

2
two
••

Squilly the squirrel

3
three
•••

Moley the mole

4
four
••••

Hug the bear

5
five
•••••

Spike the hedgehog

6
six
••••••

Help the animals with the calculations in this book.
Draw over the dotted lines and write the numbers in the boxes.

Usborne Workbooks
Adding

seven

Illustrated by Maddie Frost

Written by Holly Bathie
Designed by Meg Dobbie

Mo the mouse

Coco the raccoon

ten

eight

nine

Foxy the fox

Bun the rabbit

You can use the pages at the back of the book for writing your own calculations.

Edited by Jessica Greenwell
and Kristie Pickersgill
Series Editor: Felicity Brooks

1 more

Count how many things each animal has found then give them each 1 more. Write the numbers in the boxes.

Squilly

I love acorns.

How many acorns does Squilly have?

Draw 1 more acorn and trace over the 1.

$\mathbf{1}$

How many acorns are there now?

Mmmm, berries.

Stripe

How many berries has Stripe found?

Draw 1 more berry and trace over the 1.

$\mathbf{1}$

How many berries are there now?

Squilly now has an odd number of acorns...

...and Stripe now has an even number of berries.

odd   even   odd   even   odd

$\mathbf{1}$ $\mathbf{2}$ $\mathbf{3}$ $\mathbf{4}$ $\mathbf{5}$

Odd and even

Count the other things Squilly and Stripe have found and give them each 1 more. Circle 'odd' or 'even' under each number.

The number line at the bottom of the page can help you choose 'odd' or 'even'.

Olly

How many leaves?

odd   even

Draw 1 more leaf.

How many now?

odd   even

How many worms?

odd   even

Draw 1 more worm.

How many now?

odd   even

even   odd   even   odd   even

6   7   8   9   10

Adding more

How many clouds are in the sky?

Draw 2 more clouds.

How many clouds are there now?

How many apples are in the tree?

Draw 3 more apples.

How many apples are there now?

Who wants an apple?

Mo

Coco

Bun

1 2 3 4 5 6 7 8 9 10

Twit twoo!

When you are adding more things, instead of writing 'add', you can use the adding sign, which Olly is pointing to.

How many trees are on this page?

Add 4 more trees.

How many trees are there now?

+

Wait for me, Hug!

Foxy

Hug

How many flowers can you see?

Add 5 more flowers.

How many flowers are there altogether?

+

What is it equal to?

Mo and her friends need the same number of apples on each side to balance the see-saw.

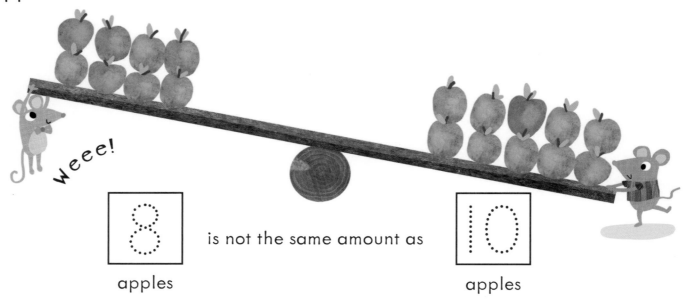

8	is not the same amount as	10
apples		apples

The mice have added 2 more apples to make the see-saw balance.

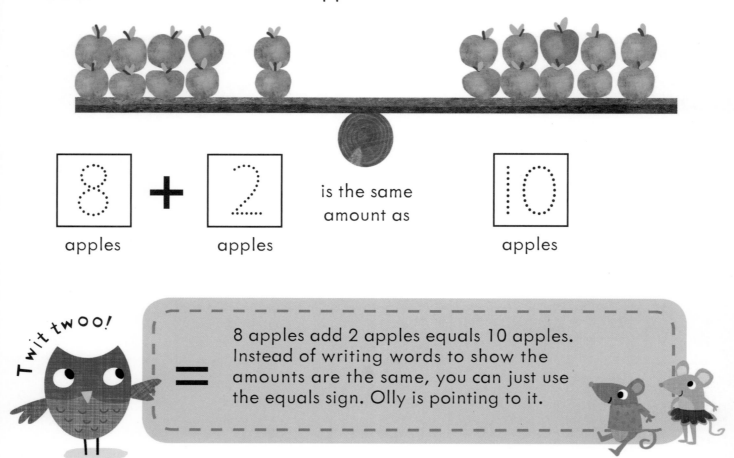

8	+	2	is the same amount as	10
apples		apples		apples

8 apples add 2 apples equals 10 apples. Instead of writing words to show the amounts are the same, you can just use the equals sign. Olly is pointing to it.

Now the mice are putting apples, acorns and stones on the see-saws.
Draw more things to make them balance and then fill in the boxes.

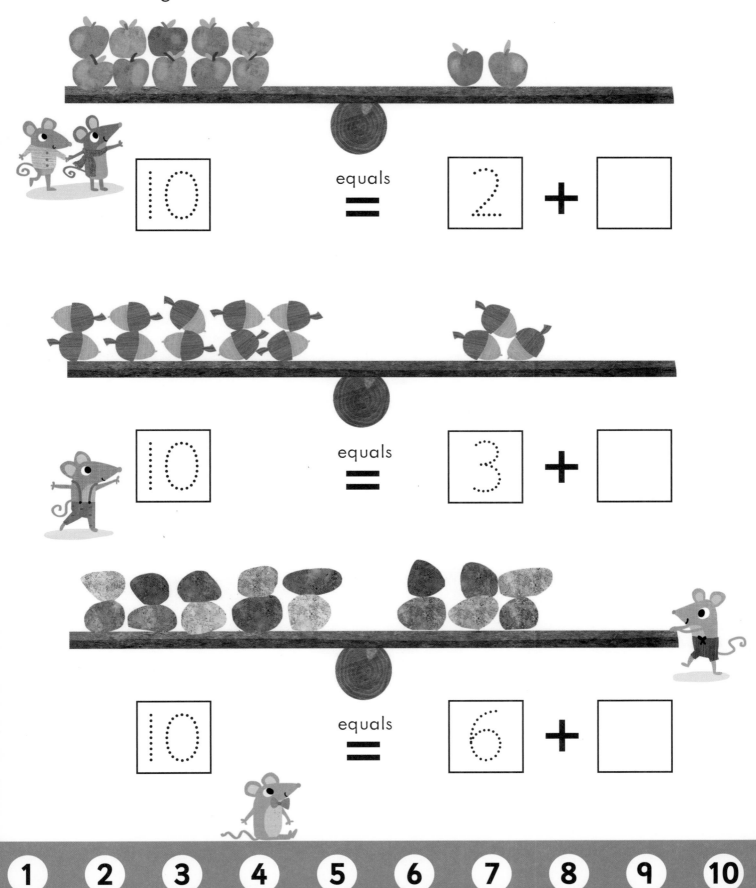

10   equals
=   2   +   ☐

10   equals
=   3   +   ☐

10   equals
=   6   +   ☐

1 2 3 4 5 6 7 8 9 10

Adding 2, adding 3

These trains will take Moley and Mo to the seaside.
Write how many animals are on each train. Then draw
the 2 friends in the windows and finish the calculation.

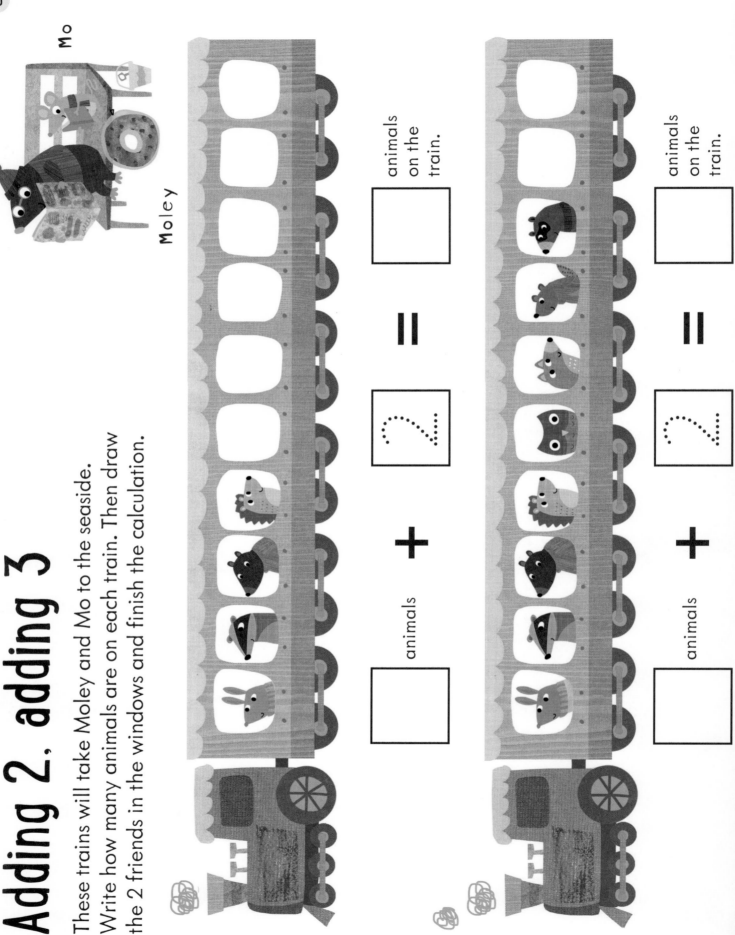

Mo

Moley

animals $+$ 2 $=$ animals on the train.

animals $+$ 2 $=$ animals on the train.

These trains will take Stripe, Foxy and Hug to the adventure park. Write how many animals are on each train. Then draw the 3 friends in the windows and finish the calculation.

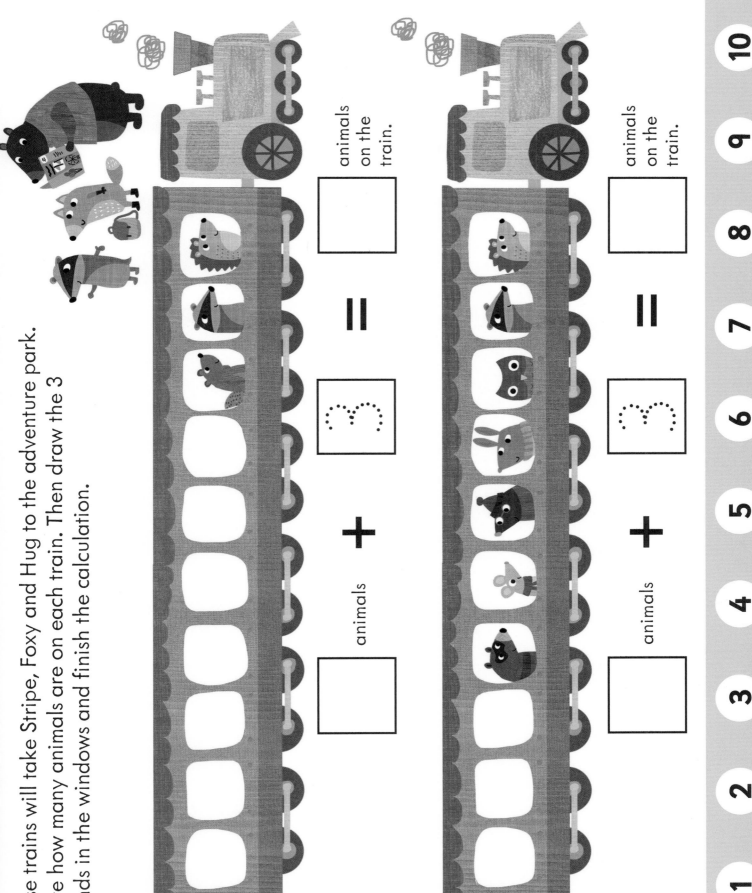

animals + ⌣⌣ = animals on the train.

animals + ⌣⌣ = animals on the train.

1 2 3 4 5 6 7 8 9 10

Adding together

The animals need help choosing rides to go on. Find two groups to fill the pony ride and draw lines to join them to it. Then fill in the boxes on the next page.

Complete this calculation for the two groups you've found to go on the pony ride.

$$5 = \boxed{} + \boxed{}$$

Find two groups to go on the teacup ride, then complete this calculation.

$$6 = \boxed{} + \boxed{}$$

Find two groups to go on the big wheel, then complete this calculation.

$$7 = \boxed{} + \boxed{}$$

Making 10

Moley has four party bags and wants to put 10 toys in each bag.
Help her to start by writing how many toys are in each group below.

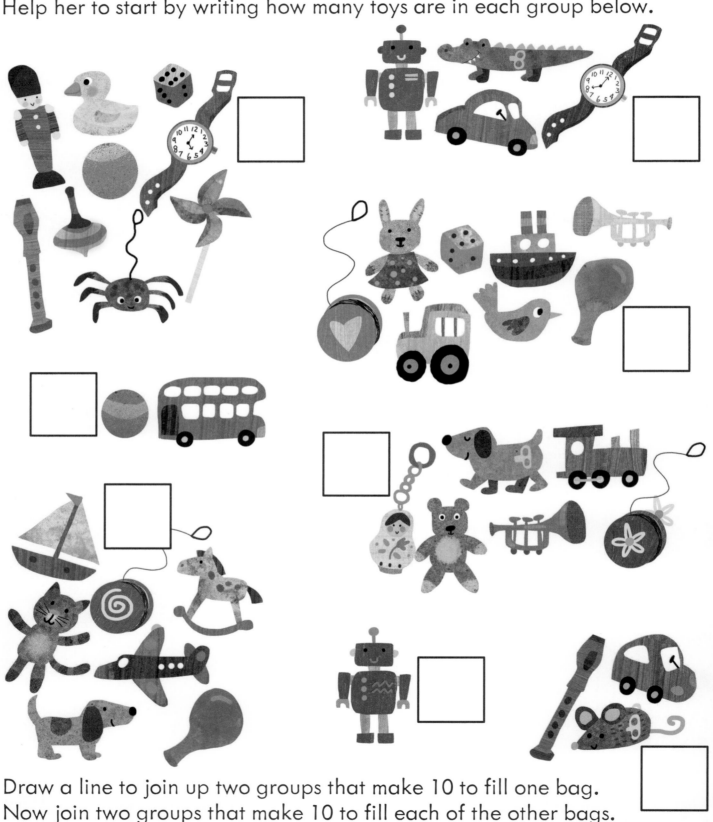

Draw a line to join up two groups that make 10 to fill one bag.
Now join two groups that make 10 to fill each of the other bags.

Now I have **10** toys in each bag. Can you help me finish these calculations?

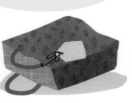  

10 = ☐ + ☐   10 = ☐ + ☐

10 = ☐ + ☐   10 = ☐ + ☐

Draw another group of balls below to make 10 and then fill in the boxes.

10 = ☐ + ☐

Finding pairs

Miss Bear wants a pair of animals to sit at each table.
The numbers on their chairs should add up to 10.
Draw pieces of string to join two chairs to each table.

Miss Bear

Can we sit together, Moley?

Who could I sit with?

Adding zero

Squilly thinks if he adds zero to any amount, that amount will stay the same. To find out if he is right, draw 10 sweets in the box below.

Now draw 0 sweets in the box and write how many sweets there are altogether.

 + **=** [ ]
sweets   sweets

Help Squilly to finish these calculations.

$9 + 0 = \boxed{}$ $2 + 0 = \boxed{}$

$8 + 0 = \boxed{}$ $6 + 0 = \boxed{}$

$1 + 0 = \boxed{}$ $7 + 0 = \boxed{}$

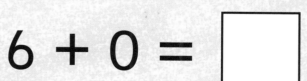
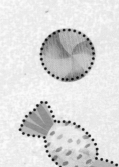

More than 10

Can you help Mo count how many tasty treats are on each tray in the bakery? Write the totals on the labels.

1 2 3 4 5 6 7 8 9 10

The mice are buying treats for a birthday party. They want more than 10 of each kind. Draw a star next to each tray that has enough treats on it.

Mmmmm, these look yummy.

11 12 13 14 15 16 17 18 19 20

More adding together

The animals are shopping in pairs at the market. Fill in the boxes to show how many things each animal has bought and how many each pair has altogether. You could count along the number line to help you.

How many pieces of fruit do we have altogether?

bananas + apples = altogether

Do we have more fruit than Moley and Stripe?

lemons + pineapples = altogether

All these oranges are heavy!

plums + oranges = altogether

Draw a star next to the pair that has bought the most fruit.

1 2 3 4 5 6 7 8 9 10

Can you help Coco complete the calculations
on her shopping list?

Things to buy

$9 + 10 =$ ☐

$10 + 7 =$ ☐

$6 + 10 =$ ☐

Good morning.

Number game

When Foxy stops the music in this game, the animals must get into pairs that equal 10. Foxy has just stopped the music – write the missing number for each pair.

Let's change the rules!

The animals play again, but this time their pairs must equal 20. Change the numbers you've written so that the pairs equal 20.

1 2 3 4 5 6 7 8 9 10

Lots of calculations

Use this page to write lots of your own calculations that equal 10.

This is fun!

 + =

 = +

 + =

 = +

 + =

Let's try some more.

Now you could try writing some calculations that equal 20. Use the space on page 31 to write them down.

Use the space on page 31 to write them down.

11 12 13 14 15 16 17 18 19 20

Adding quiz

Find out how much you can remember about adding by doing this quiz.
Answers on page 26.

A. What is 1 more than each number Hug and Foxy have written?
Write the answers in the boxes for Mo.

5
3
7
4

15
11
13
19

B. Squilly and Stripe need help sorting out these numbers.
Write each number in the correct circle.

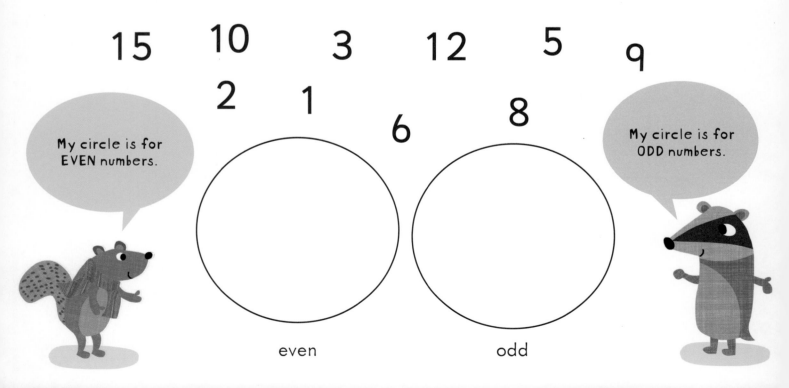

15   10   3   12   5   9
2   1   6   8

My circle is for EVEN numbers.

My circle is for ODD numbers.

even   odd

C. Spike is adding to make 10. Has he got all of his calculations right?
   Put a tick in the box next to the ones that are correct.

$9 + 0 = 10$ ☐ $7 + 3 = 10$ ☐

$8 + 3 = 10$ ☐ $3 + 5 = 10$ ☐

$5 + 5 = 10$ ☐ $7 + 0 = 10$ ☐

$1 + 9 = 10$ ☐ $2 + 8 = 10$ ☐

$2 + 3 = 10$ ☐ $6 + 4 = 10$ ☐

$4 + 5 = 10$ ☐ $10 + 0 = 10$ ☐

D. Copy the calculations Spike got wrong into the
   blank spaces below, and this time write the
   correct answers for him.

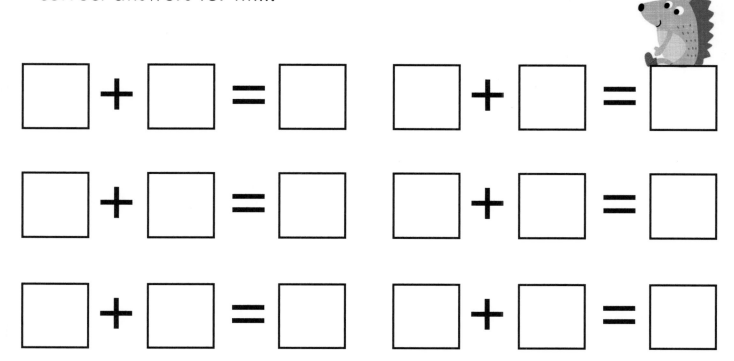

☐ + ☐ = ☐   ☐ + ☐ = ☐

☐ + ☐ = ☐   ☐ + ☐ = ☐

☐ + ☐ = ☐   ☐ + ☐ = ☐

E. Complete these calculations for Moley and Coco.

19 + 1 = ☐

4 + 13 = ☐

15 + 5 = ☐

11 + 3 = ☐

12 + 6 = ☐

10 + 10 = ☐

20 + 0 = ☐

3 + 15 = ☐

7 + 10 = ☐

17 + 3 = ☐

16 + 2 = ☐

10 + 1 = ☐

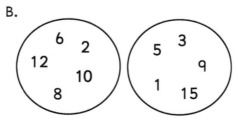

Quiz answers

A. 6   16
4   12
8   14
5   20

B.

6 2
12   10
8

5 3
   9
1 15

C. These are the ones Spike got right:

5 + 5 = 10   2 + 8 = 10

1 + 9 = 10   6 + 4 = 10

7 + 3 = 10   10 + 0 = 10

D. 9 + 0 = 9
8 + 3 = 11
2 + 3 = 5
4 + 5 = 9
3 + 5 = 8
7 + 0 = 7

E. 19 + 1 = 20   20 + 0 = 20
4 + 13 = 17   3 + 15 = 18
15 + 5 = 20   7 + 10 = 17
11 + 3 = 14   17 + 3 = 20
12 + 6 = 18   16 + 2 = 18
10 + 10 = 20   10 + 1 = 11

Score 1 point for each correct answer and write your score in this box:

42

Answers

pages 4-5

Squilly has 4 acorns, add 1 more, makes 5 acorns.
Stripe has 5 berries, add 1 more, makes 6 berries.
6 leaves, (even) add 1 more, makes 7 leaves (odd).
7 worms (odd), add 1 more, makes 8 worms (even).

pages 6-7

2 clouds, add 2 clouds, makes 4 clouds altogether.
4 apples, add 3 apples, makes 7 apples altogether.
5 trees + 4 trees makes 9 trees in total.
3 flowers + 5 flowers makes 8 flowers in total.

pages 8-9

$10 = 2 + 8$
$10 = 3 + 7$
$10 = 6 + 4$

pages 10-11

4 animals $+ 2 = 6$ animals.
8 animals $+ 2 = 10$ animals.
3 animals $+ 3 = 6$ animals.
7 animals $+ 3 = 10$ animals.

pages 12-13

$5 = 2 + 3$ or $3 + 2$
$6 = 2 + 4$ or $4 + 2$ (or $3 + 3$)
$7 = 3 + 4$ or $4 + 3$

pages 14-15

$10 = 3 + 7$
$10 = 9 + 1$
$10 = 6 + 4$
$10 = 8 + 2$
$10 = 5 + 5$

page 16

$3 + 7 = 10$
$9 + 1 = 10$
$6 + 4 = 10$
$8 + 2 = 10$
$5 + 5 = 10$

page 17

$10 + 0 = 10$
$9 + 0 = 9$ $2 + 0 = 2$
$8 + 0 = 8$ $6 + 0 = 6$
$1 + 0 = 1$ $7 + 0 = 7$

pages 18-19

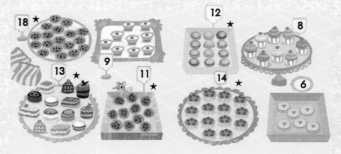

pages 20-21

$2 + 10 = 12$
$10 + 3 = 13$
$6 + 10 = 16$ ★
$9 + 10 = 19$
$10 + 7 = 17$
$6 + 10 = 16$

pages 22-23

See answers to page 16.
(and $0 + 10 = 10$)
$1 + 19 = 20$
$7 + 13 = 20$
$10 + 10 = 20$
$5 + 15 = 20$
$8 + 12 = 20$
$6 + 14 = 20$

Did you find the right answers?

28

You can use these pages to practise some adding calculations.

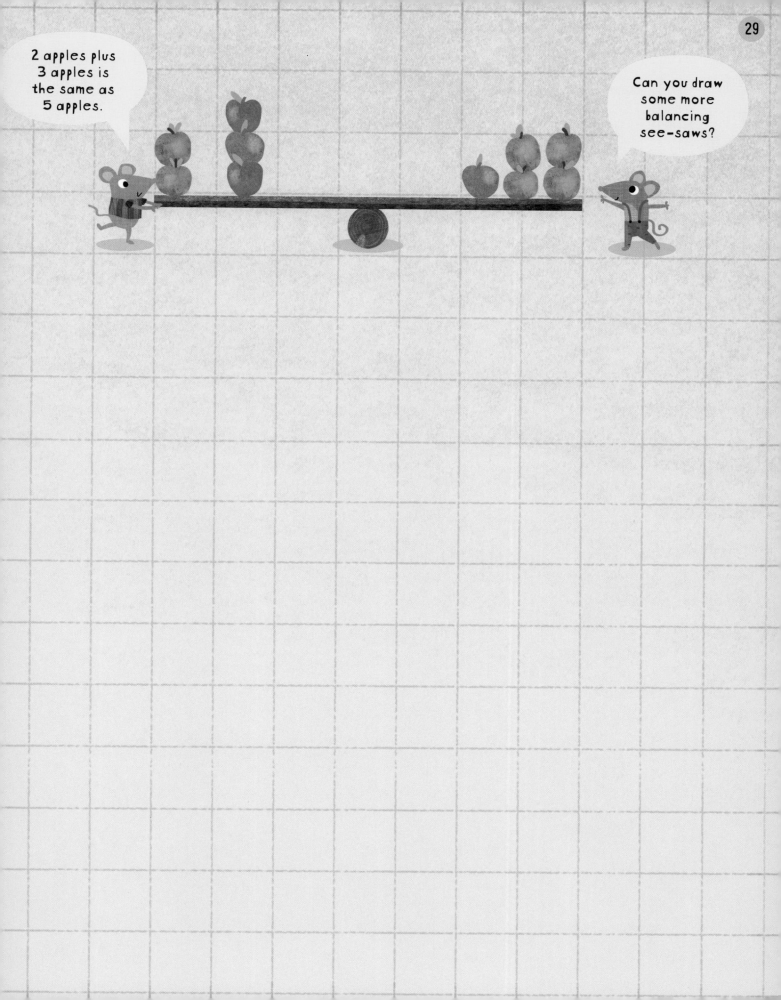

Notes for grown-ups

1 more/Odd and even (pages 4-5)

This helps children to understand that a numeral (a number) represents an amount, and that adding to an amount increases its size. The activities help them to see that numbers along the number line increase by 1 each time and let them practise identifying the odd and even numbers up to 10.

Adding more (pages 6-7)

This introduces the '+' sign. You could encourage children to count on from the first number as they draw and to use the words 'add', 'total' and 'altogether'.

What is it equal to? (pages 8-9)

This explains what the '=' sign means, and helps children to understand that two different amounts can be combined to equal a larger amount. This is what is shown by an adding calculation using '+' and '=', and why the total amount can also be put at the start of the calculation.

Adding 2, adding 3 (pages 10-11)

These pages help children see that a total can be made in two different ways. Children may also notice that adding two odd numbers together, or adding two even numbers together results in an even number. They could also find out what happens when they add an even and an odd number together.

Adding together (pages 12-13)

This activity shows children that numbers can be added together in any order. They could try swapping the position of the numbers for each calculation to check this.

Making 10 (pages 14-15)

This allows children to try finding pairs of numbers that equal 10. In maths language, these are known as 'number facts for 10'. Children could check that there are not any other pairs of numbers that equal 10. They may realize they can write a calculation using 0.

Finding pairs/Adding zero (pages 16-17)

This helps children identify number facts for 10. It's a good idea to let them practise this until they are confident. Adding zero helps them learn the value of zero – nothing – and realize that using it in an adding calculation makes no difference to the answer.

More than 10 (pages 18-19)

Children could use the number line to help with counting and forming teen numbers. They may identify numbers with two digits as being more than 10.

More adding together (pages 20-21)

These activities let children practise adding a single digit and 10 to make a teen number. They could count along the number line to help them. Check they understand where the '1' should go when writing any teen number, regardless of the order of numbers in the calculation.

Number game/Lots of calculations (pages 22-23)

This helps children recall number facts for 10, including with 0, and encourages them to understand related number facts for 20.